measures

measures

poems

b. l. bruce

Black Swift Press

ISBN-13 (trade paperback): 978-1-7357074-0-2
ISBN-13 (eBook): 978-1-7357074-1-9

Cover image by Yoann Boyer

Published by Black Swift Press.

Visit www.blackswiftpress.com for more information.

PRAISE FOR *Measures*

"As its poems tread through forests, over mountains, and along the water . . . *Measures* captivates."

— *Clarion Reviews*

"[B. L. Bruce's] newest poetry collection, *Measures*, by turns elicits tenderness and melancholy, hopefulness and heartbreak— which is to say, the gamut of the human condition. . . . Bruce's collection offers many accomplished and memorable moments."

— *BlueInk Review*

"Lyrical and reflective, award-winning Bruce's latest, a collection of poems, micropoetry, and American haiku, offers a litany of ruminations on nature, love, and self. . . . Readers seeking meditations on nature, life, love, and spiritual renewal won't be able to put [down] this perceptive, deeply engrossing read. This is a winner."

— *The Prairies Book Review*

"Lyrical poems on the beauty of the natural world contrasted against the fragile, sometimes broken nature of the human experience."

— Andrea Janda, *Visitant*

"A bittersweet journey through nostalgic memoirs, Bruce's poetry is the song we have all known while never having heard the words— until now."

— Cheriese Francoise Anderson, Author of *Wild Chai*

ACKNOWLEDGEMENTS

Special thanks to the editors of the following publications in which some of these poems, in whole or in part, first appeared:

- *The Remnant Archive* ("The Color Blue" [under the title "Miracle"] and "When I Die," September 2020)

- *Emerge Literary Journal* ("Dark Star," November 2020)

- Haiku Society of America's *Frogpond Journal* (haiku: "ice carved valley,/sun shimmer/of granite," Fall/Winter 2020)

- *Le Merle Poetry Journal* ("Full Moon at Albion River, Evening" and "Vermont," Winter Volume I)

- *Visitant* ("North," "Enterprise," and "Mockingbird," November 2020)

- *Blood Moon* ("Ration," December 2020)

- *Feral: A Journal of Poetry and Art* ("Cachagua Road," February 2021)

CONTENTS

measures

CACHAGUA ROAD

From the low bridge over the river you spoke,
blue lupines rising silently beneath the oaks,
weighed with the damp of evening.
Your words were carried away downstream,
lost to me. I felt a sadness,
heavy as stones.

I listen—bending of water
over rocks, wind in the arms
of the trees. I've learned the voices
of the robin, the towhee,
thrasher—useless except for
the way I decipher
what sounds escape from you,
which ones signal displeasure.

It's not enough to go cursing into the forest,
hope you'll come for me, then waiting—
for dusk, for signs of your tenderness,
for some bright corner
in the room of your body.

What was it you said?
Louder still, your silence hangs
over the water.

And all the while, the brown thrasher
among the sagebrush, singing.

DEVOTIONS

For weeks now, the days
have grown warmer;
shadows fall in different places.
The jay tests the angles of the eaves
and fills a pocket near
the drainpipe with twigs.

So many devotions
to otherwise nameless things:
an urgency to greet the morning
and its violet colors; let in
the air as it slips inland off the sea;
wait for the elegant shapes
of the pelicans to arrive.
On the grey beach, the plovers
skip along the wrack.
Soon, they will be leaving.

Before long, not far from here,
the fields will be tilled,
turned over and shaped
into neat lines.

MORE AND MORE

More and more
each year:
sudden lines
and marks
on my body.

MANIA

The coyote yipped
sleepless near the meadow
with such fervor I thought
impossible, feeling envy
for the way I've lost that
in myself. Bright fire
burns the quickest.
This is because of you.

The morning sky bloomed
the deep rouge I'd long admired
until it came to mean
the hint of who you'd become
when enraged, the aftermath
of the night before
when the mania clears—
how the moon lingers after sunrise
as a reminder of night.

Yet just now
near the doorway
your hand caught my elbow,
pulled me to you, lips
at my temple. This close,
we had the quiet courage
to fall apart.

SPRING HAIKU

I.

Bright morning,
ripe apricot
on the tongue.

II.

Wren's nest in the woodshed,
yellow mouths
wide and wanting.

III.

All around me
like wind:
life.

IV.

The black dog
pants from her body
new heat.

V.

Dove song—
one coo
to lure another.

LOCUST

In the days after
you took your own life
it rained without end
as though, too,
the world mourned.

And it did.
The floodwater rose,
and the earth was being buried
under feet and feet of water,
and then it was burning.

And after the pandemic spread,
after the first protests sounded
and the riots erupted,
in some place far away
the locusts came
in great swarms
and chewed away the crops,
leaving nothing.

And all this was to become
the roughed hand
of our era, the one that
smothers the mouth—
the things we don't talk about.

And when they bury you,
you become earth—
the same as them.

YELLOW

for L. and P.

What I can't forget is the sound
of that yellow warbler. Up and up
we climbed Wasatch Mountain,
poolings of snow lingering
in the shadowed valleys.
In the quiet along the riverbank
we did not speak.

Cupping our hands, drinking
the sweet alpine snowmelt,
the wind slipped through poplars,
and that warbler song echoed in the canyon.

Now, I still hear it, that colorful sound,
and think of that day upstream,
those chalk-white poplars,
high mountain wind.

GIFT

Take stock
of yourself—
how much to give,
limb by limb
chiseled away
and submitted as a gift
but not willingly.

BAPTISM, RIO DEL MAR

I thought nothing of
the man being guided into the surf,
carried through the waves,
then briefly held underwater
before emerging, soaked
and white as a ghost
except the ease with which
the bruises of his sins were cleansed
as if simply walking out of the water,
this emergence meant his being forgiven,
his resurrection.

BEGGAR

Some things
will always
imprison us,
carried like scars.

I begged my body
not to love you.

CARDINAL

After all, a body
is only salt and water
and bone—a lot of
preposterous red—

so when you
described
for me the viscera
of a human

I think a deep
Bordeaux, the hue
of the patterned suit tie
we argued over

the rouge I smear
across my lips
when wrought
with need

a yell—because even
the sound of it has a color—
to draw me from the house
to watch the cardinal

the final time I bled
and my desires
where shadowed
by your own.

Such histories
in our bodies.
How could another
learn them?

RHYTHM

Quiet mornings like these,
sun in the corner, I notice
the wide paddles of the
fiddle-leaf fig open like
so many hands unfolding.
I want each one to reach out—
touch me—think them yours,
awaken beneath their rhythm
as they tremble near the
open window. My skin
dimples in the breeze.
Air here is eddied
with silence.

RELIGION

His religion is the body
he cannot do without—
hers, not his own.

FULL MOON AT ALBION RIVER, EVENING

The swallows are tumbling
over the black banks of the river.
Above the cottonwoods
a pair of jays, their wailing feverish,
slip into the leaf-cover
then back.

Cloud cover parts briefly,
an opal-white moon bends closer,
dances in the current.
I am lost in the aphrodisia.

There isn't a word
in my native tongue
to describe something so exact:
mångata—glimmering
reflection of moonlight on water,
highway of light.

CLEAVE

The spring the starlings nested
in the attic we heard the fledglings'
stirring, the sound driving you to unrest.
You boarded up the entry and we
smelled the rot weeks after,
heavy silent of it in the rooms
like an unwanted guest.

In those days you came in from the terrace
smelling like air after the rain,
fussed about the kitchen. You wouldn't
look at me, spoke into the cupboards. Anyone
would know you were angry.
In my abstinence, I did nothing
to soften the edges of it.

And at that there was a cleaving—my heart
from yours—a finality. This
is when we divided.

CHANNEL

The headlands, green-topped
and painted pink with sea thrift,
fall in jagged heaps—
but not in wither or defeat
but in grace, after all
once stubborn and wild
rising from the wide channel.
The ocean spreads
out and out. The rule
is such that it is
either in your blood
or it isn't.

SHAME

We waded west, unspeaking,
through Gazos Creek until
it bled onto the wide beach.

I felt your eyes at my back
as I pulled at my dress,
walked into the sea.
Nothing in you
thought to stop me.

I turned to look at you,
cuffing the hem of your pants,
and thought you'd come after me,
but instead disappeared
beyond the rushes.

Later, I came for you—
through the dunes
and half-naked—
see you bent over the creek.
I caught your reflection,
and you, mine.

I saw it
flickering in you,
a word only later
I'd come to know.

AT BURNS CREEK, EVENING

I.

Sodden earth,
blue air—
the musk of out of doors.

II.

Near evening—
finch song,
clouds over green field.

III.

August dusk—
curve of moon,
bone-white.

WINTER

I watch you dream,
and outside it
begins to snow.

IN THE GARDEN

I.

Dying oak
veiled
in moss.

II.

Hummingbird
sipping
from lilac.

III.

Red hawk
on the wooden fence
eyes the mole.

IV.

Trumpet vine:
vessel
of poison.

V.

Sun setting,
white roses
fold.

IT HAPPENED ONCE

It happened once. We had tried
to be lovers long ago,
put it on, walked around,
then doffed it like a hat.

BAHÍA DE LOS ÁNGELES, BAJA CALIFORNIA

for my father

Sounds push against
the western mountains,
echo back. Long shadows
of the cardón
stretch into dusk.

Before nightfall we
bathe in the sapphire
of the gulf, drift to
sleep beside its waters,
bathed in firelight.

We dream of it—not just then,
but years after we've left—
the water's impossible hue,
salts of the shallow bay
mixing in our blood,
that knotted muscle
beneath our ribs
thumping it through us.

MEASURES

I.

All our collected things
assemble on windowsills,
in the bookcase—
such measures
of one's life.

II.

Dust gathers in the
neglected corners
where our grief settles.

Soundless rooms
become the badlands
of our desperation.

III.

The furrowing
around the eyes
comes as a reminder—
in everyone—
of age, as a season
changes
at first slowly
before we notice
then all at once.

DARK STAR

I had not expected, mid-life,
that already my shining years
would be behind me, traded
for more essential things:
what it means to have patience,
to wage a war. How one must
simply endure.

I remember clearer now:
the smooth dunes,
bare shoulders,
my body feeling somehow
less bound, belonging
to me. You came out
of the sea—salt on skin.
In a particular way,
your face opened
beneath the midday sky.
Those early days I miss
when the light in your eye
hadn't dimmed—before
you closed to me, some magic
you never spoke of
dissipating.

Yet we are here, still,
silvering at our temples and
saturated with all
we've lived, dark star
on my horizon.

VERMONT

For many years
I've not thought about
those white pillars of birch,
having traveled across the country
for the wedding of a cousin
I'd never met, sat in a small church
in a brown dress bought
for the occasion and later
thrown away.

There was nothing
of significance to recall,
less moved by the faces
of so many strangers
mirroring my own
than by those trees,
miles and miles of them,
paper-white and
straight as bones.

DECISION

Surely, by now, you see
that your indecisiveness
was a worse fate than
making the wrong decision.

SHIFT

I.

Floorboards moan
in the other room,
sound of your return.

II.

Changing hymns
of my body—
longing for yours.

III.

From my womb
a flutter,
a thirst.

WHITE LILIES

Love me, I ask of you.
Press your mouth to mine,
I want to say.
The contours of our limbs
are restless.

We throw ourselves from the house
at sundown, wander down the hill,
pass the milk-white folds of the lilies
yawning and rising along the fence.
I brush my body against theirs.

At once, the murmur of rainsound
like a stone skipped on the still pond,
braying of the great heron—
such a graceful
collection of angles crouching
in the sedges.

And before I can sing
my want to slip into
mud-smell of the dark water—
we find in this a certain rapture—
you are unbuttoning your shirt.

SUBMISSION

Do not mistake
my retreat into silence
for submission.

WHISPER

Though you deny
it ever happened
those years ago—
broad, cloudless sky,
great slab of sloping granite,
our bodies half-submerged,
roused in the river—
I remember.

The wind breathed
into the sycamore
and you, in the same
whisper, I am sure:
I love you.

EVENING HAIKU

I.

Each evening
the shifting of wings—
ravens to roost.

II.

Colder still, after sundown—
red sky in southern sky,
a swash of deep blue below.

III.

Sky-smolder to the west,
over black water:
singing loon.

IV.

Moss in moonlight,
whispering stream,
fireflies.

V.

Last of the moon,
keep count
the hours.

THE COLOR BLUE

Tell me what brings you
to your knees, what becomes of us.
Your fears.

I can tell you in my own words
what we are: we are many things—
small humors, superstitions.

It must also be said
there can be beauty in anguish—
in yours and in mine.

Each of us our own poetry,
a language of wounds, and of dawn,
and the color blue.

And aren't we, after all,
the miracle of a long-ago mess
as though by accident?

What more need we be?

LAKE WILLIAMS

It was my own image
in that still water

that set in me like stone
the form of you—

in my arms,
the valleys that

began to form
in the mattress.

Only by affirming myself
could I substantiate you.

RATION

The scent of jasmine,
whose toppling blooms
rest in a short vase,
fills the room
at the back of the house
where you go to be silent.

And when we least
expect it, there will always
be something more.
I can rely on this,
the transience
of a blue and white
California sky, of the
crowned sparrows,
their painted faces
bent upward
in pealing song.
A storm's temper
will pass. Not even you
can stay me.

I consider the moon,
the shadowed face
in certain ration,
and find relief.

BURREN MOUNTAINS, SEPTEMBER

for my mother

Those mornings
we rose early to climb
over the grey shale
lost to purple heather,
moss thick as cotton,
dip our hands
in the hillside streams,
wild as you.
And consumed by
the wind—perfumed
by the Celtic Sea—
drumming in our ears,
you raised your arms
to embrace it, let out
such joyous noise.

AUTUMN POEMS

I.

Terns fly
across the bay,
push against bitter wind.

II.

October sky
blooming:
marigold, tangerine.

III.

After rainsound,
gulls in the drafts
above the cliffs.

IV.

Gingko yellow,
cold morning air—
telling of winter.

DESTROY ME

I gave you the power
to destroy me, but
trusted you not to.

UPSTREAM

Lest we forget,
at one moment, deep,
all sterling and emerald
and in another
we press the slippery pink muscle
to our tongues for sustenance.

There is no pretending
we don't remember a story
beginning miles upstream, then down;
the spawn, the spilling into the sea.

And what, then, when there is no journey,
no sip of those wild words rising
from the stream?

We will suffer,
at first only selfishly,
then as all do.
There's not more
we can understand.

THE DESENDENT

It was autumn and a man hung himself from the trestle over the creek, the image burned into my mind: an accidental glimpse long enough to remember the slight sway, the black and white shoes suspended there in morning shadow.

To think that at some point such a decision had been made—a place high enough, the knot in the rope, a leap. Yet later the man remained unnamed—*the desendent*—as though the man's spirit merely abandoned the vessel of his body, drifted down as though he hadn't really been a man at all, as though it never happened.

FEWER

Few times in my life
I have loved.
Even fewer
are the days
I have loved
myself.

DECEMBER

For the rest of my life
I'll wonder if you've forgotten
the dance in the snow
beside the red barn.
Frost gathered on your boots.
You were fifteen.
It was late December,
and the air was still.
Snow like goose down sank
from the weighted bows of spruce.

ON DUSK

I.

Nightfall:
the long dusk
betrays me.

II.

Red sky at night:
a sailor's tale
to shake salt at.

III.

July half-moon,
light at the water's edge—
white foam.

IV.

Beyond the window:
bright orb
mistaken for the streetlight.

UNDRESS

The lupines rise and open,
send their sophisticated colors
about the meadow, then—
short lived—buckle.
What confidences would spill
from their delicate lips
should they speak?
Their blue fire a twilight,
a discernible cue that
we, too, are changing.

In that slow undress of spring,
the honeybees go
humming and powdering
themselves elsewhere.

Before long, the waxwings
will return—the *chee-chee*ing
of their opinions.
The dark and brooding
morning will return.

And later, because you cannot
slow it, the frost in the grass,
snow on the mountain.

AT ROCHES POINT

Each hour
in darkness
the ships passed,
a faint rattle
to the beveled glass
in their panes,
a yellow glow
of lights
on black water.
All the while
the steady
blink of the
lighthouse
over the narrow passage
became a melodic,
silent song
for just one instant
illuminating
the northern sea.

DUSK

The windows hang open
on their hinges.
On days such as these
there is so much to again
be moved by: soot-colored
shearwaters blurring the horizon,
the briny air of slack tide
on up-canyon wind,
the parading hours of dusk
in which you whisper, slowly,
the voice that yields me
as though I am clay.

ENTERPRISE

Heavy blooms expose
their fleshy bodies
in such enterprise
among the dunes—
as mine to yours.

Such immeasurable delight:
the pale lips of the iris
curling to the listless sky.

In its assault on the shore,
the throbbing surf
folds again and again.

Somewhere through the mist
a gull is flying low,
calling out.

WHITESBORO, SUMMER

The golden mirror
of the ocean was beginning its rise,
the sun pushing toward it.

I was struck, quite simply,
By the color of the sky—
marigold, shining—
air thick as
warm honey.

Only twice in my life
have I known such delight.
Drunk with it.

And you,
you'd missed it.

I gave up trying to describe it
when we were lovers.
And yet, I
was the worse for it.

NORTH

For a moment in the calm,
between gusts of wind:
the faint push of air beneath wing.
The northern harrier drifts above
a flowering field of yellow mustard.

Bobbing among the eddies,
the murre learn centuries
of the waterwork and currents,
driven unthinking by what
we cannot know.

Farther still, the north horizon
is choked with fog;
the clover lies trampled by salt wind
along the clifftop.

I turn my face into the sun.
Were it not for some small
burning ember,
I'd have lifted my arms
and fallen into the sea.

MORRO BAY

A woman
in the distance
stands in the gray sea,
bends to hold it
in her hands
so tenderly—
I yearned to know
such a caress.

MY MOTHER'S MOTHER

You were raised in a Boston convent,
beaten by nuns, spent long evenings,
knees in bruises, worrying the ebony beads
of your rosary before running away to California.
For most of your life that string of ink-colored pearls
was pulled through the pages of a Bible, kept hidden
in a bedside table drawer. You never spoke of your youth.

Again escaping, it wasn't the cancer that budded
in you but the undoing of your mind that won,
a plague of lost memory, a puckered scar
across your breast. I know you, mostly,
in photographs and stories, the recipes
my mother replicates. My sister wears your pearls.

But it is because of you I know well our brevity,
the evidence of it filling the room where you lay dying.

In the end, was it a blessing to forget, thinking
some sense of salvation from the peril
of hellfire and brimstone?

EVENING

The curtains flutter,
and for a moment I think
someone's dancing
across the meadow.

AND IF YOU DID

How often does your mind wander there,
that afternoon—the blue shadows
of high clouds, miles of curving
highway, and finally the sloping,
honey-colored hills?

Do you picture your pleasure
in that moment or,
knowing the stain I somehow
left on your boyhood,
your pain—perhaps disgrace,
forgetting all you once wanted.

And if you do, do you see
me as I was or all
you'd hoped I'd be?

EVERYTHING

There is only before, nothing,
and after, everything—
then, after everything,
nothing once again.

MOCKINGBIRD

As it often does
moving by memory,
your body finds mine, fits
puzzled into angles and curves
in those hushed hours—
were it not for the mockingbird
screaming into the moonlit,
slate-grey sky.

I envy you,
your unbothered sleep.
No torment. No great,
stirring voice
in your mind
screaming,
screaming.

IMPATIENCE

In such consuming want I am impatient.
This I know to be true.

Is it too much to want someone
to love me enough to beget more of me,
to recreate me?

TO FORGIVE

From the paddock near the willows
the ewes bleat their way
across the meadow,
small moons of dew
cling to the wildrye.

Twice this morning I stopped to listen:
geese bellowing, gliding inland
toward the marsh.
That same bitterness returned,
the kind that held me
beneath its demanding paw.

And only until, finally, my resolve melted
did I try to free myself. Yet,
I've still not learned to forgive.

ALPINE POEMS

I.

Red clay,
syrup-smell of pine,
treeline mirrored in the still lake.

II.

Blue mountains
rising in the west,
snow-shouldered.

III.

Ice-carved valley,
sun-shimmer
of granite.

IV.

High alpine stream,
deep sapphire,
your dappled skin.

WHEN I DIE

When I die, burn my body. I hope to leave with you—
among other things—a sort of fury, enough for you to
imagine me beating the ground with my fists, igniting.

ABOUT THE AUTHOR

Award-winning author and Pushcart Prize nominee, California poet Bri Bruce (writing as B. L. Bruce) has been called the "heiress of Mary Oliver." With a bachelor's degree in literature and creative writing from the University of California at Santa Cruz, her work has appeared in dozens of anthologies, magazines, and literary publications, including *The Wayfarer Journal, Canary, The Remnant Archive, Northwind Magazine, The Soundings Review, The Monterey Poetry Review*, and the American Haiku Society's *Frogpond Journal*, among many others. Bruce is the recipient of the Ina Coolbrith Memorial Poetry Prize and the PushPen Press Pendant Prize for Poetry, as well as the author of four books: *The Weight of Snow, 28 Days of Solitude, The Starling's Song,* and now *Measures.* Her highly praised debut collection *The Weight of Snow* was the 2014 International Book Awards poetry category finalist and the 2014 USA Best Book Awards poetry category finalist. *The Starling's Song* was released in February of 2016, and was selected as Honorable Mention in the Pacific Rim Book Festival. In addition to her writing pursuits, Bruce is also a painter and photographer, with work that has been featured in *The Sun Magazine, Near Window*, and others. Follow her on Twitter @the_poesis and on Instagram @thepoesis.